40 Days of Conversations with Her

Practical Conversation Starters For the Busy Man

Shawn McBride

40 Days of Conversations with Her

Copyright © 2023 by Shawn M. McBride

ISBN 9798391487395

Table of Contents

Introduction 1

Day 1 4

Day 2 5

Day 3 6

Day 4 6

Day 5 7

Day 6 7

Day 7 7

Day 8 8

Day 9 8

Day 10 9

Day 11 9

Day 12 10

Day 13 10

Day 14 10

Day 15 11

Day 16 11

Day 17 12

Day 18 12

Day 19 12

Day 20 13

Day 21 13

Day 22 14

Day 23 14

Day 24 15

Day 25 15

Day 26 16

Day 27 16

Day 28 16

Day 29 17

Day 30 17

Day 31 17

Day 32 18

Day 33 18

Day 34 18

Day 35 19

Day 36 19

Day 37 20

Day 38 20

Day 39 20

Day 40 21

Conclusion 21

Shawn McBride Teaching Resources 23

Introduction

40 Days of Conversations with Her

Through my years working with couples, I have realized that the most essential thing in a relationship is not sexual attraction. It is not the personalities or temperaments of the individuals. Still, it is time they spend TALKING with each other. If you are not talking together, one of you will be walking out sooner or later.

Most men do not understand that talking and sharing make a woman feel closer and more connected. This is a need for women, not just a want. If you want to enjoy a more meaningful and abundant sex life, you will invest time talking and connecting with her each day.

Before I go any further, let me tell you something to help you understand why this is so. Women equate sex with love. If they feel loved, sex for them is a joy. Men do not necessarily look at sex in this way. For men, it's a need, not a bonding thing.

Think about the time when you first met your lady. You could not get enough of her and would talk to her for hours. You spoke of the most essential things in your life and silly things without meaning. Those hours of talking helped you to get to know one another and discover a deeper connection. But for most men, this is a mating ritual; the courtship will get them to their needs.

It has been said that a man should talk to his lady for at least 15 hours each week (about 2 hours a day). Let me say that again. A man should speak to his lady for at least 15 hours weekly. Before you start to mumble about that amount of time, I want you to recall that when you were trying to win her love, you spent more than 15 hours a week giving her the attention she deserved. While she is the same lady, she still needs and deserves your undivided attention in a quantity that lets her know she is unique and you are devoted to her.

Those hours of conversation should be done face-to-face without interruption. Still, I understand that life does not always give us that luxury. Suppose you work away from home, or you each work different shifts. In that case, you may have to occasionally allow telephone conversations to substitute for face-to-face. However, now we have FaceTime.

Two hours daily can be broken down into 3 twenty-minute segments or 4 fifteen-minute stretches. If you are both busy working, your talk time may happen in the morning over coffee, in the kitchen after you clean up in the evening, or on the porch. At the same time, you unwind at the end of the day or lie in each other's arms at night. Just make sure you give her your full attention, listen to what she says, and engage in conversation. Don't view this as a duty or chore. If you do, your mind will wander to all the other things you could be doing, and you may resent the time you're spending with her. Your attention will be divided, and you may miss out on some of the wealthiest parts of your woman.

Look her in the eye. Pay attention. Validate what she is saying by appropriately responding. That doesn't mean nodding your head to show you're paying attention. It doesn't mean just blindly agreeing with everything she says. It definitely does not mean she needs or wants to be fixed. Sometimes, women need to vent. For example, you ask her how her day went, and she tells you her boss is a jerk, he doesn't understand the workload she's under, and so on. But you love your job, you respond. Yes, I do, she says, but he's still a jerk. So, quit. That's your solution. To you – the man – it's a problem solved. You've come up with what you believe is the obvious fix for the problem. Wrong. She was only venting. She wants to be heard to get it off her chest and get over it. You could respond with something funny like I'll hold him down while you beat him. She might laugh at that. Now it's a problem solved.

You must also speak in complete sentences and not in one-word grunts.

You can initiate these little daily talks by asking questions that start them. Remember that each conversation, each hour you spend, will increase your understanding of your lady. They will also increase her appreciation and fondness for you.

The key to a 50-year marriage that is happy is not money, worldly items, or earth-shattering sex. The key is to talk and share ideas and feelings, allowing you to bond closer to each other than anyone else on Earth.

Day 1

You can begin this entire exercise with a simple question set.

Don't just ask her how her day was. This is vague and can lead to a one-word answer: Good, rotten, or okay. Which only tells you a little.

Better: Did anything good happen today?

This is going to give you insight into things that bring her joy. Engage in whatever it is, even if you don't understand it. Try to see her there, or you there with her. Mentally bring yourself into the event or happening.

For example, she went out to lunch with friends. Sally's purse was on the floor next to her chair. She was quietly dropping tea bags from the restaurant into her purse. When they got up to leave, Sally picked up her purse and realized she had been missing it. All the teabags were on the floor. That might not sound funny to you, but it was a hysterical moment for the girls.

The other side of that question can work to continue the conversation. Also, open a discussion with this if she is in a noticeably lousy mood.

Not so good: What happened today that made you feel bad?

Better: Did something miserable happen at work today?

Listen carefully to her answer because she is about to reveal something that causes her emotional trauma or grief.

You have the conversation rolling, and now it is your turn to tell her something that made you feel good or bad that day. Emotional sharing is a two-way street; you must ensure you meet her there. However, as a friend died, I caution you not to steal the limelight, especially if something terrible has happened. Although that's extreme, you get the idea. You are not necessary at that moment. Marriage is only sometimes 50-50. Sometimes it's 100-0.

If it's appropriate, tell her something that happened that made you feel bad. You are allowing her to know you on a deeper level. A way to connect to you and strengthen her feelings for you. Men often don't share feelings, but if one of your friends badmouthed another, for example, you might feel he was being disloyal, which really bothers you. Let her know. She'll see a side of you that matters to you.

Keep this give-and-take conversational tone throughout the rest of these daily questions. I've given you the question. It's up to you to make it warm, friendly, and personal, not interrogative.

Day 2

Today's question will give you insight into what your partner wants to create their idea of a perfect day. For some of us, an ideal day is spent doing nothing; others might find a perfect day filled with activity. Listen closely and remember what she says as she imagines her perfect day for you. You can open the conversation by telling her you'll take notes to plan some great days in the future. She'll appreciate that you want to remember what she says.

When it is your turn to answer the question, be honest. Do not just say what you think she wants to hear. Tell her what your perfect day would be like; you might enjoy some of the same activities, like playing golf all day or going to a mile-long yard sale. But your day might be simply watching football. Don't cover this up, or you'll end up becoming resentful.

Q. What would your perfect Saturday be like?

Q. What is your most trivial favorite thing to do on Saturday? Every guy eventually ends up with a honey-do list. If something around the house needs urgent care, do it. But if your perfect day does not include home repairs or mowing the lawn, let her know. You're entitled to at least one free weekend a month!

Day 3

Knowing what movie a woman loves to watch can tell you more about who she is and what she dreams of. Do not assume that she is going to love romance movies. Many women are into action and suspense.

By knowing her favorite movie, you can choose entertainment in the future that you can be sure she likes. This question sounds irrelevant, but you connect to your lady on a deeper level by understanding what gives her pleasure, even if it is a movie.

Q. What is your favorite movie?

Q. What is your favorite movie?

Ask her *why* this is a favorite movie. It might not be that it's an action movie or a comedy. For example, it might be her favorite because she loves Brad Pitt in this movie. Or because she loves the musical score, the scenery, or the film editing.

Day 4

This question set is a little deeper, but it is meant to give you a glimpse of how your partner thinks about their gender and the opposite sex. We spend so much time discussing how equal men and women are we forget there are significant differences between the two sexes other than the physical.

When you answer this question, open up and tell her what you love about being a man and what you hate about being a man. True intimacy can only be developed between couples who share and bond ultimately.

Q. What is the best thing about being a woman?

Q. What is the worst thing about being a woman?

The answers may surprise you both, leading to exciting and eye-opening conversations.

Day 5

You might think that Christmas is the favorite holiday of all women. You could be surprised by your partner's answer. She may love Easter, Thanksgiving, Labor Day, or Halloween the most. The holiday she loves the most is connected to fond memories of that day. This question can lead to you learning more about her childhood and what shaped her into who she is today.

Q. What is your favorite holiday? Why?

Q. What is your least favorite holiday? Why?

Day 6

Where in the world would you go if you could go anywhere? This question opens up a channel into her dreams and ambitions. Would she like to see another country, would she want to go to a famous landmark, or would she prefer to go to a mountain top? How she answers this question will help you to know what you can do to encourage her and help her achieve some of her dreams and fantasies.

Q. Where would you go if you could go anywhere in the world without restrictions on money or resources? What would be your favorite way to travel there?

Q. Name one place you would never want to go. Why?

Day 7

If you want to know what your lady is all about, you need to know what she is most passionate about. Her passions are part of what drives her, and when you know her passions, you can see what common grounds the two of you share. Her passions will tell you how to motivate her and give you a look at not only the woman she is but the woman she will be in the future. And don't forget to ask "why" after each question. Understanding why someone wants or needs something goes more profound than the one-word answer.

Q. What are you most passionate about?

Q. What is something you cannot tolerate?

Day 8

Our past and those who helped shape us are essential to our futures. This question lets the two of you explain who in your lives touched you deeply. The connection may have been with a teacher, a pastor, a grandmother, or anyone else. This is an opportunity to discover more about what she found inspiring and comforting in her past and what made her feel safe and loved.

Q. Who in your life influenced you the most? Who made the biggest impression on you? Q. Why does this person stick in your mind so much? What was it about them specifically?

You can do the same with a past event. Ask her: "What sticks in your mind the most about a significant event in your life?"

Ask about negative impressions made by people in her past or events that caused negative emotions. Why did it bring up such an emotion? Talking about these things can clear out a lot of suppressed resentment, fear, shame, or other negative emotion that often comes up at the wrong time.

Day 9

Everyone has a talent or a gift. Some people can cook, some can paint, some are good athletes, and others are natural-born caregivers. You know what things your lady is best at doing, but it may surprise you to find out what *she* thinks she does best.

Finding out what she struggles with will help you connect and allow you to help her in the future. This information can increase your knight in shining armor appeal.

Q. What is something you think you are really good at?

Q. What is something you think you could do better? Would you ever want to get better at that, or does it just not interest you?

Day 10

This is different from knowing what her favorite movie is. Her favorite movie is tied to a message she likes. Her famous actor or actress will typically be someone she admires. Actresses often choose their roles to get a piece of news to people. Your partner will select her favorite based on the kind of person she thinks the actress is and not just on the roles she portrays.

Q. Who is your favorite actor or actress? What is it about them that you admire?

Q. Which actor or actress is your least favorite? Why?

Day 11

Suppose you understand the answer to this question. In that case, you will have an emotional connection to your partner that is stronger than steel or titanium. What day would your partner choose to live over again? Was it a happy day, and she wants to experience the joy, or was it a sorrowful day, and she has regrets and would like to make changes?

This profound question will require her to bear part of her soul with you. Please do not take this lightly, and be tender with her feelings.

Q. If you could go back in time, which day would you like to live over again?

Q. Why? Is there something you would change about that day?

It was enough to explore and reminisce if this was a good day. If it's a sad day, you'll be exploring feelings that are not easy to go through again. You may need to express that there is nothing she could have done differently. But again, don't try to 'fix' her. Just let it be an organic experience that comes through her.

Day 12

On a slightly lighter note, you can learn much about a person by knowing their favorite gift. Not only does the answer to this question help you treat her and pick out future presents, but it also lets you see what she values most. You are likely to be very surprised by this answer.

Sharing similar values is great for a relationship. Knowing your partner's values will let you see if you share similar tastes and values. You are about to discover if your partner prefers the simple, understated items or if she prefers something more of an attention grabber.

Q. What was the best gift you were ever given? What did you love about it?

Q. What was the worst gift you were ever given? Why did you dislike it?

Day 13

This is another question that can reveal the values your partner has, or it can show you what things touch her deeply. How she would give away this money lets you know what things are dear to her heart and what changes she would like to make in the world. The answer to this question will help you to see her giving and nurturing nature.

Q. If you had $5000 to donate or give away, who would you give it to? What about this group or person draws your heart over the many other possibilities?

Day 14

Is your lady someone who prefers to cuddle before a fireplace or lay in the sun listening to the waves? Suppose you want to connect with her emotionally, sexually, and in every way. In that case, you have to know what she would prefer to do.

The answer can help you comfort her and excite her. When it's your turn to answer this, ensure she understands what you prefer and *why* you prefer it.

Q. Do you prefer the mountains or the beach? What feelings and emotions does a beach bring up for you? Or the mountains? What is it about them that conjures this feeling?

Day 15

Discussing what snacks you loved as children will bring up memories of happy childhood experiences. The goal is to make your lady feel relaxed, secure, and content. Childhood was a time when the majority of people did have those feelings, especially when they were eating their favorite childhood snack.

You can also learn something you can use later to give her a treat when she least expects it. Remember what her favorite snacks were and what they are today.

Q. What was your favorite snack as a child? This is one of the more fun questions because it opens up all kinds of childhood memories. You'll laugh together and maybe even wonder why those memories came up!

Q. What is your favorite snack today? Tastes change as we get older. What you both loved as kids might differ significantly from what you enjoy today.

Day 16

People give us advice almost every day of our lives. Some of that advice is good, and some of it is not. Talking about the best advice she was ever given will allow her to open up and share an experience with you. Even if the incident was not pleasant at the time, she would have you here with her now so she could bring it out into the open.

She will be showing you her vulnerable side. Be careful and resist any inclination to be judgmental or critical of her during these discussions. When you are talking, she should feel safe. You may not think this is a vulnerable area. Still, the best advice she's received might have been constructive criticism that, at the time, felt hurtful and was only later perceived as good advice. You want her to feel like she can tell you anything and that you will listen, understand and love her through it.

Q. What is the best piece of advice someone has ever given you? Who gave it to you? Why did they offer this advice at that particular time? Has that advice affected any decisions since then? Each of these additional questions can help to further the conversation.

What is the worst piece of advice someone has ever given you? Why was it bad advice?

Day 17

There is some skill or craft that each of us wishes we could do. Asking her to reveal the art or skill she wants to learn is asking her to open up and share her private thoughts and secrets.

These questions bring about conversations like you had when you first met. Women connect through conversations. They feel more intimate towards you when you share long talks and expose emotions to each other.

Q. Is there some skill or craft you would like to master? Is there something you want to pursue on your "bucket list?"

Day 18

This topic can open up some deep discussions. Most of the time, when someone hates to hear a misconception repeated as a fact, it is because they, or someone they are close to, are touched by it.

You will find a deep area of emotion and experiences that your partner may have been keeping bottled up. You may see where you have common ground or discover some of their secret hurts and anger. It can also help you avoid future arguments because you unwittingly repeated that misconception.

Q. What common misconception do you hate to hear repeated as a fact?

Day 19

This topic requires you and your partner to look deep into yourselves and share emotional trauma. Being bullied is traumatic, whether it happens as a child or an adult. Most people stuff those old feelings and fears deep inside themselves because they are painful. Often, people are ashamed they were bullied. This is a discussion that is going to draw you closer because you have to expose things you may not want to reveal. Be honest when it is your turn to share. When you show your lady your vulnerable side, she will think more of you, not less. Open up and let her see some of your emotional scars, and you can work on healing them together.

Q. Have you ever been bullied? Intimidated? Shamed?

Q. Have you ever bullied someone? Have you ever been mean because you were in a bad mood and took it out on someone else?

Day 20

These questions and some talking will draw you closer to your partner. You want a deeper relationship and more intimate relationship. Intimacy does not mean sexual, but when a woman feels the closeness and intimacy that she can only share with someone she trusts, she will be sexually attracted to that man.

You need to know what she loves and hates. Where she dreams of being in five years and the past that shaped her. We have something that makes us smile every time we see it. It might be a baby goat, a child playing, or a favorite movie.

The answers to these questions will connect you and your lady in a very intimate way.

Q. What makes you smile no matter how often you see or hear it?

Q. What makes you cry no matter how often you see or hear it?

Day 21

Our past should never be held against us. It has shaped us into who we are and how we respond today. One of the beautiful parts of childhood is the magic of Santa Claus. This question is fun and is meant to help you understand how your lady has matured emotionally.

Her belief in something that cannot be seen, heard, or touched demonstrates her ability to believe in your relationship even when times get tough. When you answer this question, try to be open and honest. It is a fun topic, but it reveals much about you both.

Q. Did you believe in Santa as a child?

How did you find out he wasn't real?

This conversation can also extend to things that cannot be seen, heard, or touched: God, spirit, energy, ghosts, the afterlife, the Easter Bunny...

Day 22

Most people had one friend in their childhood who was their best friend. This was the friend you trusted and could say anything to. You carry this friend in your heart throughout your life because you bonded with them so closely.

This question makes your lady share the intimate details of her best friend. The enemy question is an extra, but knowing who hurt your lady in the past and how they dealt with it can help you understand her.

Q. Who was your best friend as a child?

Q. Who was your worst enemy as a child?

Day 23

There are no right or wrong answers to any of these questions. There should be no judgment applied to any of the solutions. These are means of opening conversations that help you grow as a couple. There are going to be ideas and values you share, and because you are not the same person, there will be ideas and values you disagree on.

It is okay if your lady's thoughts and dreams differ from yours. Variety is the spice of life. The little differences will keep you interested in each other and provide opportunities to learn and grow as a person, friend, and lover.

Q. Would you rather live a boring life for 100 years or an adventure-filled life for 60 years?

Day 24

Our fears reveal so much about us. Your lady will have to trust you before telling you her greatest fear. You may know that she is scared of spiders or thunderstorms. Still, her greatest fear is something she keeps inside herself because she fears that telling someone about the fear might make her vulnerable.

This question is best asked when you are close enough to hold her or, at the very least, put your arms around her. She needs that physical closeness to feel safe enough to share this with you.

Q. What is one thing you always wanted to do but were afraid to try?

Q. What is it about our world today that you literally fear?

Day 25

How we have been impacted by the events of our life often puts our lives on different paths. This question will reveal a lot about your lady, why she thinks the way she does about certain things and her expectations for the future.

When you answer this question, be sure that you are as open and dig as deep as she does for the answer. The two of you are establishing an intimate bond, and the solutions you are giving will provide the other person with the ability to comfort you, give you more joy, and understand how you feel about things.

Q. What single event in your life impacted you the most? Ask whether this was a negative or positive event and how it affected her decision-making and worldview afterward.

Day 26

A flower is something that almost every person will say is pretty. Does your lady like daisies' clean, fresh look, a rose's soft, velvety feel, or tropical flowers with bright colors? Knowing her favorite flower allows you to surprise her with bouquets in the future, giving you more insight into her nature.

Is she more playful, more serious, or more romantic? The woman's nature reveals what you can do and how you can approach her so that she is more receptive.

Q. What is your favorite flower? Why? Is it the fragrance, the petal's feel, the color, the way it grows (straight up, drapey, or in clusters...)

Q. Which flower do you like the very least?

Day 27

This is another profound question that shows you the things and the people your lady finds essential. Whom she would choose to sit with for the hour can reveal past regrets, past loves, or an inquiring mind looking for answers to life's questions.

Q. If you could sit with one person from the past for an hour, who would it be? What would you like to ask them? Does the person you would like to sit with change every few years?

Day 28

This question is fun and reveals a little more about what your lady likes. Maybe she has a guilty pleasure in watching old sitcoms or likes to indulge in decadent chocolate or long bubble baths. Knowing the answer will make it easier to always please her, cheer her when she is down, and understand her.

Q. What is one of your guilty pleasures? Or are there several I should know about?

Day 29

If you were on a desert island, and one song played the entire time you were there, what song would you want it to be? This is a fun question, but a romantic might choose a love song, and the young at heart might pick upbeat music they could dance to.

This question lets the two of you be silly and share some surprising insights about what you like.

Q. What would it be if you could only hear one song for the rest of your life?

Day 30

This is a fun question. Would your lady prefer to be invisible, extremely strong, able to leap tall buildings in a single bound, or have some other superpower? What would motivate her to choose certain powers, and what would make her not want other powers?

This simple question can open hours of discussion about possibilities and what you could do "if." Learn a little more about what your lady would like to do. You may be surprised at some of the answers you hear.

Q. If you could have a superpower, what would it be?

Day 31

This is another one of those questions that you should make notes on. She is about to tell you the breakfast foods that could make her day the best day possible. You are about to learn little things that could please her immensely. Remember these answers!

Q. What would your perfect breakfast look like?

Q. What do you least like to eat for breakfast?

Day 32

This is another question that opens up her feelings, her desires, and her fantasies. If she wants to dream about something, you can tell the bank that this is important to her.

The dream that would make her feel comforted, happy, and relaxed holds the key to what makes her tick, which is the key to learning how to make her happy. The nightmare she is scared to relive tells you what demons and fears she has lurking and how to comfort her and chase those demons away.

Q. What would you dream about if you could choose your best dream?

Q. Is there one nightmare you hope to never have again?

Day 33

Getting to know your lady means you need to get to know her family too. You do not just marry a woman; you marry into a family. What do they like to do together -- as a family? What are their interests, and how does your lady relate to her family? Are they close? Remember, this is the family that helped shape her.

Knowing these things will explain why she is the way she is. It can also give you a lot of laughs and help you avoid future arguments.

Q. What is the strangest thing your family does?

Q. What is your favorite family tradition?

Day 34

You may think you already know the answer to this question, but you may be surprised if you hear a different response than the one you expected. This is the one question that can teach you more about how to please her in the future and how to choose the perfect date night restaurant.

You will also learn that she might have pretended to like certain foods in the past to please you. Women often do that. Make her understand that you want to know her favorites to grow together.

Q. What is your favorite restaurant or food type?

Q. What is your least favorite?

Q. Is there some food you've never tried but would like to? (Let's go out this weekend and try it.)

Day 35

You have asked her what makes her smile, but a laugh-out-loud moment differs from a smile. What was the last thing to make her laugh out loud? This is a fun and silly question, but it is also a way to discover how your lady's mind works and what tickles her funny bone.

Women are often attracted to men who can make them laugh. They want men with a good sense of humor. Here is your chance to learn more about her sense of humor.

Q. What is the last thing that made you laugh out loud?

Q. What is the last thing that made you cry?

Day 36

This next question is about body image, something many women struggle with. The answers to this question will tell you more about what she thinks about herself and what you can do to bolster her self-confidence. Do not tell her that you believe her button nose is cute. Think about why she does not like it and try to understand that.

The answers to her body image issues will also guide you when making love. If she is self-conscious about her belly, you will know ahead of time and cannot draw her attention to her stomach during intimate sessions.

You will also learn what things she may need to be complimented on more. If she hates her hair, you may need to praise it.

Q. If you could change your features, which would you choose?

Q. What is your favorite feature?

Remember, this is a give-and-take. Please share your own insecurities with her.

Day 37

This answer can guide you in the future so you can plan a perfect day for her. What event has she attended that she loved? What events has she attended that she would never have gone to?

You are beginning to know what makes your lady who she is and how to keep her happy.

Q. What is the best event you've ever gone to? What did you enjoy about it so much?

Q. What is the worst event you've ever gone to? What made it the worst event? Was it a poorly planned event, or was there something about it that made you uncomfortable?

Day 38

This next one is a pretty deep question. What drives her? Why does she get up and do what she does every day? Knowing what makes her want to forge ahead – what motivates her -- even though sleeping in would be more comfortable tells you more about her as a person, her emotions, and what she would like to have in a relationship and with a man.

Q. What motivates you to get up every morning? If you need to know her long-term or short-term goals, ask her if she has any.

Q. What one thing makes you dread getting up?

If you have children, they will likely come in as part of the answer to both these questions. Listen carefully, and think about how you can take some of the load off her in this area if necessary.

Day 39

This is just a fun question allowing you to talk to her and learn more about her. What teen trend did she love, or was there a particular food she would like to eat again that is no longer on the market. There may have been values in her past that she would like to see displayed more.

The answers to this question can take you down many paths of discovery and reminiscing.

Q. If you could bring back one popular thing from your teen years, what would it be?

Q. What was the worst trend when you were growing up?

Day 40

You are asking her to open up and tell you the one thing she wants the most out of life. You are asking her to reveal to you who she is and who she wants to be. You're asking for a glimpse into her soul, dreams, and ambitions. She may feel vulnerable opening up in this way.

Show her you are willing to share emotions when it's your turn. Please demonstrate that you accept her as she is and as she wants to be. You are becoming her most trusted and valued friend, lover, and confidant.

Q. What is your most significant life goal?

Q. What do you consider the lowest point in your life?

Conclusion

Congratulations. You have completed 40 days of conversations with your lady. Your relationship is now closer than it has ever been. You know more about your lady to understand and meet her needs.

You have demonstrated to your lady your level of commitment in your relationship. You have become a friend, soul mate, and someone she will always want to have by her side and in her corner.

You have taken an essential step in creating a commitment that will last through time. A commitment that is fulfilling for you both. One your friends and families will talk about for years to come.

Now that you are connected more intimately, spend time talking to your lady daily.

Mindset Reset
ISBN: 978-1092500227
Mindset Reset is a practical book that will teach readers eight core principles of mindset renewal that will significantly enhance their lives.

Handling Life's Struggles
ISBN: 978-1986754071
This 31-day devotional will inform, inspire, and impact the lives of every reader currently facing any life adversity.

The Power of Words
ISBN: 978-1514330388
Readers will discover the importance and necessity of speaking positive words of affirmation into young people's lives and find the dangers and ramifications of speaking words of death.

Beware of Bad Company
ISBN: 978-1484850039
Beware of Bad Company is an eye-opening and practical book for people of all ages. It offers vibrant, sensible teachings on the importance of evaluating relationships.

How to Become a Successful Student

ISBN: 978-1505437607

American children spend at least 16-20 years receiving formal education. How To Become a Successful Student enlightens young people with 26 practical and easy-to-remember principles from A-Z that will help them excel in this journey.

Know Your Worth

ISBN 978-1495453939

Know Your Worth is an empowering & inspirational 365-day devotional book written to help teenage girls grow in wisdom and understanding about issues relevant to all stages of their lives.

The 5 Needs of Every Teenager

ISBN 978-1548093532

Far too many young people today feel disconnected, ignored, and completely alienated from parents and adults. After 25 years of working with adolescents, Shawn McBride authored this important book to enlighten parents and caring adults on what teenagers need relationally and emotionally to connect.

Shawn McBride's 52 Object Lessons

ISBN 978-1088489000

This book teaches you to harness the power of object lessons for those who follow you, whether they be your children, the children of others, or adults longing to know and understand the Lord.

The 5 Steps to Achieve Your Big, Hairy, and Audacious Goals
ISBN 979-8656384407
This book will inspire, challenge, and teach anyone with the inner desire and internal ambition to go hard after their BIG GOALS, BIG DREAMS, and BIG DESIRES!

40 Days with Jesus
ISBN: 979-8640215441
40 Days with Jesus was written to help Christians form the habit of daily devotion to learning from our Lord & Savior. Because the words of Jesus are life-changing and timeless, the 40 daily lessons focus only on the words he spoke.

Mannerisms – How to Effectively Respect Your Man
ISBN: 979-8638944186
Mannerisms offer women invaluable knowledge by detailing what RESPECT looks like to a man. This includes practical advice, empathetic knowledge, deep insights, and helpful solutions for women seeking a more effective connection with the man in their life.

Ladies First – How to Effectively Love Your Lady
ISBN: 979-8729153893
Ladies First offers eight practical, life-changing, and action-packed principles and explains what it looks like for a man to continue passionately pursuing and effectively loving a woman throughout a lifetime. Finally, a man can understand how to love her!

Recovery From Infidelity Workbook

ISBN: 979-8535776613

The Recovery from Infidelity Workbook is a highly effective and practical workbook designed specifically for couples seeking to save their relationship. This workbook is for couples who desire to work through the causes, ramifications, and healing from unfaithfulness, extra-marital affairs, adultery, and post-infidelity in a cathartic way.

Communication and Resolving Conflict Workbook

ISBN: 979-8549195554

Are you dating, engaged, or married and in a seemingly endless cycle of unresolved problems in your relationship? *The Couples Communication/Conflict Resolution Workbook* will help you develop new SKILLS and polish the old SKILLS you need to keep your relationship alive.

66 WAYS TO SHOW HER AFFECTION

ISBN: 9798371024787

Male readers will learn to develop new habits to show affection for their wife, girlfriend, or partner. At the start of relationships, we all experience that fresh glow that drives us to show our adoration through communication, gifts, and even displays of affection. As relationships mature, life, work, family, and other things erode away those initial feelings. We often find ourselves stuck in ruts. We get busy trying to get through the day as best we can, and relationships can wane. This book is the tool you need to refocus on your relationship and show her daily affection.

11 Most Common Reasons Men & Women Cheat
ISBN: 9798392028610

If you have ever been cheated on, you know how painful infidelity can be. In the agony of the betrayal, you ask yourself, " Why?" The Most Common Reasons Men and Women Cheat addresses this question.

Infidelity is not about a broken relationship. It is about a fractured partner. Someone who is looking for answers in the wrong places. The 11 Most Common Reasons Men and Women Cheat examines why adulterers make their choices.

If you have been in a relationship victimized by infidelity, this book will give you a better understanding of why they had an affair.

All materials are on sale on Amazon in paperback and Kindle versions or by visiting our online store @ www.CouplesCounselingCenter.org

Contact Shawn McBride, MA Licensed Professional Counselor

The Couples Counseling Center
PO Box 20 Davidsonville MD 21035
Phone: 301-615-4510
Web: www.CouplesCounselingCenter.org
Email: shawnmcbridecouplescounselingc@gmail.com
Facebook: Couples Counseling Center
Tik Tok: ShawnMcBride74
IG: Couples_Counseling_Center

Made in the USA
Middletown, DE
15 May 2023

30498659R00020